TO MÁXIMO TONATIUH,
A TEACHER AND A WARRIOR

SOLDIER FOR EQUALITY

José de la Luz Sáenz and the Great War

Duncan Tonatiuh

Abrams Books for Young Readers, New York

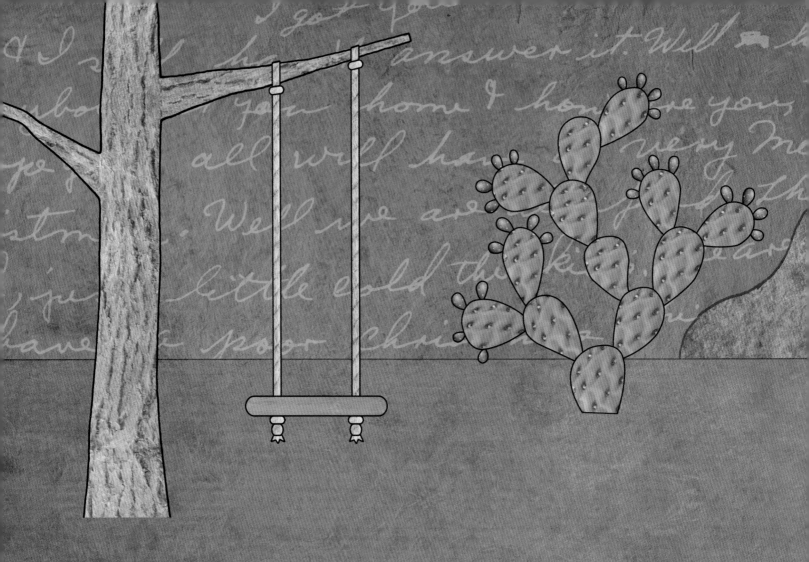

"Greaser!"

Luz (*looz*) ran toward the boy and tackled him to the ground. Luz had had enough. *¡Ya basta!* Why did they call him names? Why were those kids mean to him just because his family had come from Mexico?

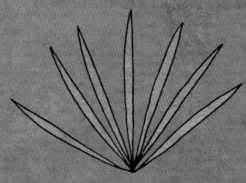

Señor Sáenz was not happy that his son, José de la Luz, had been in a fight again, but he understood his frustration. He too was not always treated with respect. Luz's *abuela* had come to the United States more than twenty-five years ago. Luz and his brothers and sisters were born here. The family was as American as the kids who tormented him!

Luz knew that people of Mexican origin worked hard just like everyone else. They worked in offices, in schools, in the fields, on railroad tracks, and in mines. But many people in Texas—where Luz was born—mistreated them. *Tejano* children were forced to attend separate and inferior schools. Businesses had signs that said NO MEXICANS ALLOWED.

"Luz, I don't want you to fight," said his father, "but don't let anyone make you feel ashamed. You should always be proud of who you are, *mijo*."

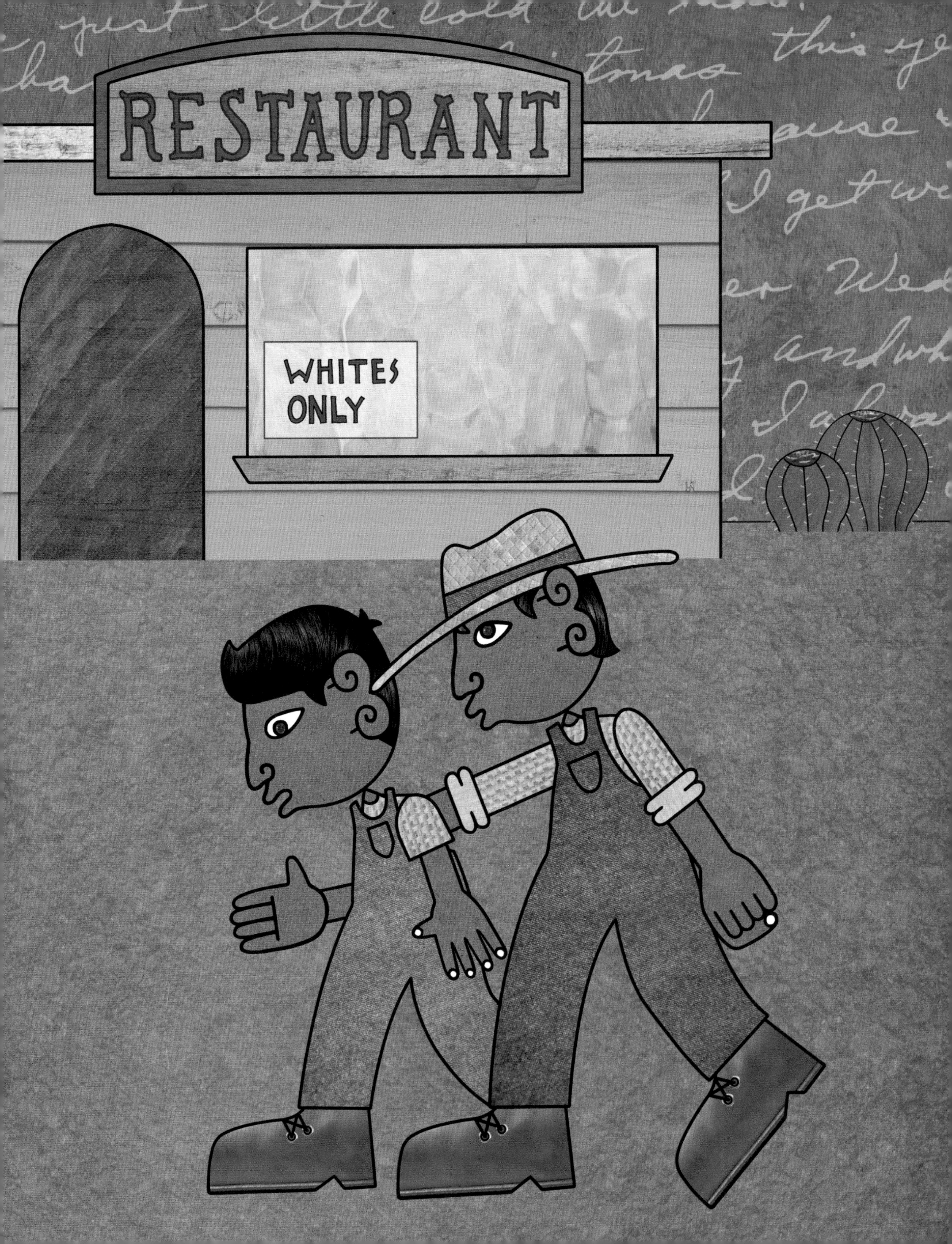
RESTAURANT
WHITES ONLY

Luz never forgot what his father said. His teachers and family friends also encouraged him to feel proud of his roots. He graduated from high school in Alice, Texas, in 1905. He then attended a school to become a teacher.

Luz knew that knowledge was a weapon that helped you defend yourself against those who were mean to you and ignored your rights. He wanted to make sure kids understood this too.

Luz married María Petra Esparza and they started a family. At a school near San Antonio, he taught kids in the morning and adults who did not know how to read at night. His students were of Mexican descent like him. Luz enjoyed teaching them, but he felt frustrated too. His school was a small shack. The school the white children attended was larger and nicer. *No es justo.* It was not right. *Will things ever change? Is there anything I can do?* thought Luz.

One day, in the middle of the school year, Luz did not show
up to class. He had volunteered to join the army. In 1914 much of
Europe was at war. Great Britain, France, Russia, and the other
Allied countries were fighting against Germany and the Central
Powers. In April 1917 the United States joined the Allies. It was to
be called the Great War, or World War I.

After saying goodbye to his family, on February 25, 1918, Luz arrived at Camp Travis, a military facility where thousands of men from Texas and Oklahoma trained to become soldiers. Luz joined the army because he believed it was his duty to serve his country. He wanted to demonstrate that Mexican Americans loved America and would give their lives fighting for it. *After they see the sacrifices we are willing to make, the people who mistreat us will start treating us fairly—*con igualdad y justicia.

While he was at training camp, Luz met Americans of different backgrounds. He met Native Americans from Oklahoma. They also faced discrimination and hoped for a better future after they fought in the war. Luz was excited when he met other Mexican American soldiers. He made many friends but became especially close to Eulogio Gómez and Eduardo Barrera.

Luz was happy to be training. He got along with most of his fellow soldiers regardless of their backgrounds. But he had negative experiences too. The worst was when an officer called him "greaser" in front of others and laughed. *This army will fight against tyrannical rulers and injustice in Europe,* he thought. *How is it possible that some officers here can be so unfair to their own countrymen?*

On June 6, 1918, after more than three months of training, Luz and the other soldiers from the 360th Regiment of the 90th Division of the US Army began their journey to the war. They traveled on a train to New York City, where they boarded the ship *Olympic* and headed to Europe.

The trip across the Atlantic Ocean was not easy. The soldiers were tightly packed belowdecks. They slept in hammocks next to one another. Luz often felt seasick. At night he thought of María Petra and their children at home and wrote in his diary: *I hope they are proud of me and that my efforts help them and others like us. Espero que estén orgullosos.*

The 360th Regiment landed in England on June 21. From there they boarded another ship that took them to France. They did not go right away to the French front where the fighting was. Instead they were sent to Rouvres–sur–Aube, a town where the soldiers received additional training.

In his spare time Luz studied French. He understood a lot of the language because it had some similarities to Spanish, which he knew perfectly. After some weeks he was able to read French with the help of a dictionary. Some soldiers teased him. "Do you think that speaking French to the Germans will stop their bullets?" But it wasn't long before other soldiers were bringing Luz newspapers so he would translate for them the news about the war.

On August 18 the 360th Regiment began marching to the front. When they arrived in the Saint–Mihiel region they saw for the first time the infamous trenches that soldiers had dug to protect themselves from enemy attacks.

Luz met soldiers there who were exhausted
from the constant gunfire, rain, mud, and cold.

Before it was Luz's turn at the trenches, he was called to a fortified command post in the rear. A colonel needed someone to translate a French message. Luz did so with ease. The colonel was satisfied with his work and assigned Luz to the intelligence office. There Luz would receive communications, translate messages, and relay them to others.

That night Luz wrote in his diary: *August 24. Now that I am in a hole thirty feet under the ground, I can tell my friends that books literally helped me build a protective trench around me.*

Although Luz was not in the trenches, he was still in danger. German planes dropped bombs on the 360th Regiment, some exploding very close by. Things were not easy for Luz at the intelligence office either. Luz often felt frustrated that he did not receive the credit he deserved for his work. *No es justo.* Was it because he was Mexican American? *I am a plain foot soldier, but I serve in a position that is for commissioned officers. If I am capable of doing the job, why not promote me in rank, not for self-serving reasons but to be fair?*

At night, while trying to sleep, Luz could hear the cannons thunder when the artillery units fired at one another. "If we survive," he later told Gómez and Barrera, "we should create an organization that looks after the soldiers of Mexican origin that fought in this war."

In France, Luz saw many men fall in combat, and others die from wounds and illnesses at the field hospital.

When he learned that Pepé González, a fellow Mexican American soldier, had died, he hurried with Gómez to the funeral. They went to the army's makeshift graveyard as fast as they could. By the time they arrived González was already buried. Luz decided to write a letter to the man's father.

"Mr. Doroteo González . . . we offered a prayer by his grave, and asked that his sacrifice not have been in vain, but that it contributes to the betterment of our poorly appreciated people."

weeks after arriving, the 306th Regiment was part of a successful battle in the Saint-Mihiel region. The German army began to retreat. Over the next month and a half, the Allies kept advancing and gaining territory. Although Luz carried a rifle, a bayonet, a dozen grenades, and hundreds of rounds of ammunition, he had not fired a single shot. He and the other soldiers in the intelligence office were ordered not to by their superiors. Their job was to receive communications and relay them to others. On November 10, however, Luz was told to get ready. The next day the American forces were going to engage in their largest attack yet. Every available man was going to be a part of it.

That night Luz could barely sleep. At dawn he and the rest of the soldiers would charge toward the enemy. They would not have any cover against the Germans' gunfire. Luz knew thousands would die trying to overpower their opponents.

"Sáenz. Sáenz! Wake up!"

It was still dark when a soldier woke Luz up and told him to report to the intelligence office. He learned that Germany had asked for a ceasefire. The major assault the American forces had planned was canceled. At 11:00 a.m. on November 11, 1918, the

Although the combat stopped, the war was not officially over.
Germany had asked for a ceasefire so that the different nations
involved in the war could negotiate peace terms. Some American
forces were going to stay in Europe while the negotiations took
place. Instead of being sent home, Luz received orders to join the
march to Germany.

The 360th Regiment arrived at Zeltingen, Germany, on December 22. Luz spent Christmas and New Year's there. He saw a town covered in snow for the first time! It didn't snow like that back home in Southern Texas. During the day Luz worked in the intelligence office. In the evenings he began teaching English to Mexican American soldiers he had met who could not speak the language well. *I have to help my own*, he thought. Tengo que ayudar a mi gente.

Luz had met many soldiers of Mexican descent during his time in the army. He wanted to bring them all together so they could share their experiences. On March 3, 1919, he organized a gathering of all the Mexican Americans in the 360th Regiment. More than fifty soldiers came. They ate and told stories. They talked about families back home. And they discussed creating an organization once they were back in the States to fight for their rights. Luz even gave a speech. "Our hearts should be filled with satisfaction," he said, "because Mexican Americans risked their own lives to fulfill their duty." *Debemos sentir orgullo.*

On May 17 the men of the 360th Regiment left Germany and began their trip home. When they arrived in San Antonio they were greeted by their families and loved ones at the train station. Luz embraced María Petra and their children, who were waiting for him eagerly.

American soldiers of different backgrounds paraded through South
Flores, Commerce, Alamo Plaza, and some of the major avenues in San
Antonio. Thousands of people watched. Luz saw friends, fellow teachers,
and even those he didn't know cheering for him and the other soldiers. As he
marched, Luz noticed that the ground was covered with flowers. *Everyone is so
happy and grateful to have us home!* thought Luz. He was filled with joy. *Alegría*

Luz's happiness faded quickly. He returned to the classroom to teach and realized that things had not improved for people of Mexican origin after the war like he had hoped they would. Mexican American children were still being sent to separate and inferior schools. Businesses still had signs that said NO MEXICANS ALLOWED.

It was time to bring to life the idea of an organization to fight for the rights of Mexican Americans. The veterans he already knew were ready to join him. Other people of Mexican origin who lived in Texas wanted to join Luz too. "I did not fight in the war," said one of Luz's friends, "but I supported the war effort. I worked extra hard in the fields so that the soldiers could have the food they needed. I even bought a Liberty bond to help the government fund the army. We did our part. Why are we still being mistreated? *Queremos igualdad y justicia.*"

There were war veterans of Mexican origin in other parts of Texas who were also organizing. Two of them were Manuel Gonzales and Alonso Perales from San Antonio, who helped form the Order of the Sons of America and the Sons of Texas. Luz met with them and they agreed to help one another. In the years to come, the three men as well as other Mexican American civil rights leaders wrote articles and traveled throughout Texas to give speeches. They worked hard to get more people involved.

Eventually Luz and the others decided to unite and create one large organization so it could have more impact. "I am convinced," said Luz during a speech, "that we should create one single union."

"It will give us the opportunity to claim our rights," said Perales, "which is the best thing we can do for our children."

On February 17, 1929, ten years after the war had ended, at a convention in Corpus Christi, Texas, the League of United Latin American Citizens (LULAC) was born.

Luz remained a member of LULAC for many years to come. The organization was involved in several cases that helped end the segregation of Mexican American and Latinx children from all–white schools. Luz continued writing articles and giving speeches to fight against racism and prejudice. He wanted the signs that said NO MEXICANS ALLOWED to disappear. Luz had proudly fought with the United States Army in Europe for the ideals of democracy and justice. Now he fought on the home front in Texas for those same ideals: *democracia y justicia*. He fought for equality. *Igualdad.*

Author's Note

The Great War—as it was called when it began, or World War I, as we refer to it now—was a brutal and complicated conflict. A number of books have been written about it and its many players but few have been written about the thousands of soldiers of Mexican descent who fought in the war.

I first learned about José de la Luz Sáenz when I met Emilio Zamora, a professor of history at the University of Texas in Austin. Through his research of Tejano history, he came across Luz's diary, which was first published in Spanish in 1933 under the title *Los Mexicano-Americanos en La Gran Guerra*. He and Ben Maya translated the diary into English, and it was published in 2014. As far as historians know, it is the only war diary published by an American World War I soldier of Mexican descent. The diary is extraordinary because it gives readers a window into the lives of Tejanos, both in the armed forces as well as those at home, and provides insight into the discrimination that people of Mexican origin experienced. Throughout his diary Luz writes about his experiences and challenges during the war, but also about the injustices back home. Luz chose to join the army even though he could have secured an exemption. He did so because he wanted to fight against tyranny in Europe, but also because he saw his service as way to fight for the ideals of equality and justice in America.

When he returned to Texas after the war Luz resumed teaching. He was a teacher for nearly forty-five years. He taught in many schools; first in the San Antonio area and later in the McAllen region. After his return he quickly realized that things for Mexican Americans had not improved like he had hoped. But rather then feel despair, he felt emboldened. Other veterans and the Tejano community at large felt the same way. Luz wrote articles, gave speeches, and became involved with several organizations that supported the rights of veterans and Spanish speakers. Most notably, he was a cofounder of the League of United Latin American Citizens, which today is the largest and oldest active Latinx civil rights organization.

Much has changed in the last hundred years. Schools are no longer legally segregated. Businesses do not display "No Mexicans Allowed" signs. But much needs to change still. People of Mexican origin and other Latinxs living in the United States continue to fight against stereotypes and prejudice.

Latinxs have proven themselves to be as patriotic as other Americans, but their service and sacrifices have often been ignored. They have fought in every American war since the Civil War. They continue to serve today. A 2015 Pew Research Center study found that 12 percent of all active-duty personnel of the U.S forces were Hispanic. But a 2016 study by the CASABA group, a Hispanic veterans organization, found that only a very small number of Latinxs reach top positions. There are 37 four-star generals in the military—the highest rank—but none of them are Latinxs. Out of 144 three-star generals—the next highest rank—only 2 are of Hispanic heritage. It is a problem that frustrated Luz a century ago when he fought in the Great War and which frustrates us still today.

Throughout this book I call José de la Luz Sáenz "Luz," which is how his family and friends referred to him. In Spanish *luz* means "light." I find it poignant because throughout his life Luz tried to shine light on the injustices that people of Mexican origin experienced. I hope this book accomplishes something similar and that it shines *luz* on a largely unsung hero whose fight for equality is still alive.

Luz's Words

The quotes on pages 15, 19, 21, 23, 28, 29, and 37 are direct quotes from Luz's diary and from the speech he and Perales gave at the 1929 Corpus Christi unification convention. The rest are not precise quotes but come from sentiments he expressed throughout his diary.

Select Timeline of the United States' and Luz's involvement during World War I

July 28, 1914: Austria-Hungary declares war on Serbia a month after the assassination of archduke Franz Ferdinand by Serbian nationalists. At the time different nations in Europe had alliances with one another. After that first declaration of war, many more followed. There was a domino effect and two main groups emerged: the Allies lead by France, Britain and Russia and the Central Powers lead by Germany, the Ottoman Empire, and Austria-Hungary. At the time Luz was teaching near San Antonio.

May 7, 1915: The United States remained neutral for the first years of the war. But after a German submarine sinks the passenger liner *Lusitania* during a crossing from New York to Liverpool, England, killing 128 Americans, the sentiment among US citizens and their government begin to change.

1916: Luz marries María Petra Esparza.

February 1, 1917: Germany had halted its unrestricted submarine warfare, but it begins its attacks again in an effort to stop supplies from coming to England.

February 3, 1917: The United States cuts diplomatic relations with Germany.

April 6, 1917: The United States declares war on Germany.

June 7, 1917: The commander of the American forces, General John J. Pershing, arrives in England with his staff.

June 24, 1917: The first US combat forces arrive in France.

September 1917: The 360th Regiment begins to assemble at Camp Travis.

February 25, 1918: Luz arrives at Camp Travis after receiving a letter that told him to report for duty.

May 28, 1918: US forces participate in the Battle of Cantigny. It is the first independent American operation in the war.

June 6, 1918: Luz and the 360th Regiment leave Camp Travis and begin their trip to Europe.

June 23, 1918: Luz and the 360th disembark at Le Havre, France.

July 1 to August 18, 1918: Luz and the 360th Regiment receive additional training at Rouvres-sur-Aube.

August 23 to October 10, 1918 : Luz and the 360th Regiment are at the front line in Saint-Mihiel.

September 12, 1918: US forces, including the 360th Regiment, attack the Saint Mihiel salient successfully.

September 26, 1918: The Meuse-Argonne campaign begins. It is a major Allied offensive.

October 16 to November 1918: Luz and the 360th Regiment are near Verdun, in the Meuse-Argonne region.

November 11, 1918: Germany signs the Armistice. Some US troops stay in Europe while peace negotiations take place.

November 30, 1918: Luz and the 360th Regiment march to Germany.

December 22 to May 17, 1919: Luz and the 360th Regiment are stationed in Zeltingen, Germany.

January 18, 1919: Peace conference begins in Versailles, outside Paris.

May 16, 1919: Luz and the 360th Regiment begin their trip home.

June 17, 1919: Luz and the 360th Regiment arrive in San Antonio. They parade in the streets to much fanfare.

June 21, 1919: Luz is discharged at Camp Travis.

June 28, 1919: Allied and German representatives sign the Treaty of Versailles. The United States does not sign the treaty but pledges to defend France in case of an unprovoked attack by Germany.

SELECT TIMELINE OF THE LEAGUE OF UNITED LATIN AMERICAN CITIZENS (LULAC)

LULAC, which Luz helped form, is the largest and oldest active civil rights organization that serves the Latinx community. These are some of its most significant accomplishments.

February 17, 1929: LULAC is established in Corpus Christi, Texas.

1931: LULAC attorneys and members assist in the Salvatierra v. Del Rio Independent School District case, the first lawsuit that challenged segregated "Mexican" schools in Texas.

1933: LULAC participates in rallies, and along with other organizations, is key in the creation of the Liga Defensa Pro-Escolar, later known as the School Improvement League, which fought for better schools and better education for Latinxs until 1956.

1946: LULAC supports the Mendez v. Westminster case. After the Mendez family and the other Latinx families involved in the case won, California desegregated its public schools. It was the first state to do so.

1947: LULAC protests on behalf of Felix Longoria, a World War II veteran from Three Rivers, Texas, who is not allowed to be buried in a whites-only cemetery. After the public outcry, he is buried at Arlington National Cemetery in Washington, DC.

1948: LULAC files the Delgado v. Bastrop Independent School District lawsuit. It is joined by the American GI Forum. Their efforts eventually lead to the end of segregated schools for Mexican American students in Texas.

1954: LULAC attorneys involved in the Hernandez v. the State of Texas lawsuit argue in front of the Supreme Court against the systemic exclusion of Mexican Americans in juries.

1968: LULAC creates the Mexican American Legal Defense and Education Fund (MALDEF).

1975: LULAC forms a National Scholarship Fund which is still active today.

1987: Attorneys file the LULAC v. INS class action lawsuit to demand that the Immigration and Naturalization Service process eligible amnesty applicants who had been denied the right to do so.

2003: LULAC settles the LULAC v. INS lawsuit successfully.

2005: LULAC attorneys challenge gerrymandering in Texas. In the LULAC v. Perry case, they argue that the legislature's redistricting plan violated the Voting Rights Act and hurt Latinx representation.

2006: LULAC, along with many other organizations, helps mobilize millions of people to march in different parts of the country for the rights of immigrants.

2008: LULAC helps register more than 50,000 voters for the general election.

2009: LULAC supports the nomination of Sonia Sotomayor and works with different coalitions so that she can become the first Latina US Supreme Court Justice.

2018: LULAC has approximately 132,000 members throughout the United States and Puerto Rico. It provides approximately one million dollars in scholarships to Latinx students each year. It has forty-eight employment training centers that provide job skills and literacy training.

SELECT BIBLIOGRAPHY

Bernal, Rachel. "Latinos aren't reaching top military positions, study shows." Casaba Group (July 22, 2018). https://www.casabagroup.net/campaign-1/

Christian, Carole E. "Joining the American Mainstream: Texas's Mexican Americans during World War I." *Southwestern Historical Quarterly* 92, no. 4 (April 1989): 559–595.

Hale, Nathan. *Treaties, Trenches, Mud, and Blood.* New York: Amulet Books, 2014.

"Hispanics in the U.S. Army: History." US Army. https://www.army.mil/hispanics/history.html

José de la Luz Sáenz Papers. Benson Latin American Collection. General Libraries. University of Texas at Austin.

League of United Latin American Citizens website. https://lulac.org/

Parker, Kim, Anthony Cilluffo, and Renee Stepler. "6 facts about the U.S. military and its changing demographics." Pew Research Center (April 13, 2017). http://www.pewresearch.org/fact-tank/2017/04/13/6-facts-about-the-u-s-military-and-its-changing-demographics/

Ramírez, José A. *To the Line of Fire!: Mexican Texans and World War I.* College Station: Texas A&M University Press, 2009.

Sáenz, J. Luz. *The World War I Diary of José de la Luz Sáenz.* Edited by Emilio Zamora. Translated by Ben Maya. College Station: Texas A&M University Press, 2014.

"Timeline (1914–1921)." Library of Congress. https://www.loc.gov/collections/stars-and-stripes/articles-and-essays/a-world-at-war/timeline-1914-1921/

Zamora, Emilio. "Sáenz, José de la Luz." *Handbook of Texas Online.* Texas State Historical Association (December 8, 2015. Modified January 26, 2017). https://tshaonline.org/handbook/online/articles/fsa97

Index

Glossary

abuela: Grandmother.

Alegría: Joy or happiness.

con igualdad y justicia: With equality and justice.

Debemos sentir orgullo: We should feel proud.

democracia: Democracy.

Espero que estén orgullosos: I hope they are proud.

mijo: A contraction of mi hijo, "my son." It is used as a term of endearment.

No es justo: It is not fair.

Queremos: We want.

Tejano: A resident of Texas of Mexican or Hispanic descent. At times the term has been used to differentiate between those whose families have lived in Texas for many years and newly arrived immigrants. More recently though the term has been used to include both. In this book I use it to mean the latter.

¡Ya basta!: No more!

The illustrations in this book were hand drawn, then collaged digitally. I photographed some of Luz's letters and included his handwriting as a texture in the background of several spreads.

Cataloging-in-Publication Data has been applied for and may be obtained from the Library of Congress.

ISBN 978-1-4197-3682-7

Copyright © 2019 Duncan Tonatiuh
Book design by Steph Stilwell

Published in 2019 by Abrams Books for Young Readers, an imprint of ABRAMS.

Printed and bound in U.S.A.

10 9 8 7 6 5 4 3 2 1

Abrams Books for Young Readers are available at special discounts when purchased in quantity for premiums and promotions as well as fundraising or educational use. Special editions can also be created to specification. For details, contact specialsales@abramsbooks.com or the address below.

Abrams® is a registered trademark of Harry N. Abrams, Inc.

José de la Luz Sáenz, US Army photograph 1918

ABRAMS The Art of Books
195 Broadway, New York, NY 10007
abramsbooks.com